TRUMPLETHINSKIN AND THE GIGANTIC PEACH

*except for Trumplethinskin

TRUMPLETHINSKIN AND THE GIGANTIC PEACH

Martin Treanor

DEDICATION

Martin Treanor—for it is still he—is grateful for the capacity to draw on those parts of his own pea-like brain that spew forth nonsense, tomfoolery, and downright malarkey. The ability of his psyche to dwell in absurdity never ceases to amaze him.
When he gets it to work, that is.

And thank you to those who bought The Tales of Trumplethinskin books. Your continued interest is very much appreciated.

It was the darkest night in *Not Far Far Away Enough*. In the woods surrounding Trumplethinskin's thick-walled house at *Mangy Logo*, owls hooted, poor and foreign-looking people were walking around just as they liked, and Trumplethinskin felt anything but safe as he sat on his bed, eating beautiful chocolate cake, hugging his roly-poly belly.

In his favorite storybook, *Fibber Fox's Tall Tall Tales*, Chucky Dollson had written the tallest tale of them all, about how people like Trumplethinskin—who actually owned golden toilets—needed to be aware and constantly terrified of the woodland fairies called *Congressters*, who lurked amid the trees.

The scariest of these was the brave brownie, Dancy Nancy, who lived in a bigly big boot, along with Cortenzel with her glowing flowing hair, the Fairy Godwarren, and the Princess Omar, who were all female Congressters, and the type that scared Trumplethinskin more than anything.

Chucky Dollson said they were telling fake news about poor old Trumplethinskin. Things like how he was stiffing everyone out of their very last magic bean to buy more golden toilets and portraits to hang above his growing number of four-poster beds. Which was true, but Trumplethinskin didn't want anyone to know about it . . .

. . . which made it fake news—or as the Wicked Witch Skellyann called it, "*alternative facts*"—because a lot of people (people who liked Daddy Trumplethinskin's big bulging bag of magic beans) had said that Trumplethinskin was the bestest best ruler the realm had ever known, and the town criers proclaiming anything else just wasn't fair at all.

"Wah – wah – wah," Trumplethinskin bawled and bawled and bawled.

Trumplethinskin cried a lot that day, but not as much as when the realms-folk discovered that he was asking other realms—mostly the evil pixie Pootie Poot's Kingdom of Rushes—to do him favors. It was meant to be secret. But some people were bad at keeping secrets, like when he'd sneaked into Stormilocks's not-too-soft and not-too-hard bed, and Mikey the Grass, who was supposed to be his loyal attorney elf, blabbed the whole story to everyone.

There were, of course, other secrets, too, like when he Peeping Tom'd at the Pageant Princesses, but that—as with so, so many other things—is another story altogether.

Anyway, as it happened, the Biden Goat Gruff—who was friends with Trumplethinskin's archest enemy, the handsome Prince Obaming—was skipping around the place, reaffirming the fake news.

And this made Trumplethinskin mad—and sad.

"Wah – wah – wah," he bawled and bawled and bawled again.

The Biden Goat Gruff was being mean and Trumplethinskin would get his creepiest, craziest elf, Ghouliani, to do something about it right now.

So off Ghouliani went to the distant land of SugarRain and, even though it would break the oldest, most important rule in the hundreds of years that *Not Far Far Away Enough* had existed . . .

. . . he warned the Kazar of SugarRain that if he didn't make-believe bad things to say about the Biden Goat Gruff, he wouldn't be allowed to dip into Daddy Trumplethinskin's big bulging bag of magic beans.

At this point, it must be revealed that, from the very beginning, the big bulging bag of magic beans wasn't Daddy Thumplethinskin's at all, but belonged to all the people of the realm, although they never got to see any of it because Thumplethinskin spent it on playing golf and having lavish balls with the Tight-fisted Turtle, Hennity Bennity, Chucky Dollson, and all the other hangers-on who gave him anything he wanted, as long as they didn't have to share any of their own bulging bags of magic beans.

As it happened, however, Ghouliani's efforts didn't work. And that was why the town criers were going around proclaiming that Trumplethinskin had broken the realm's most important rule. Which he really had. But he didn't like them saying it.

"Wah – wah – wah," he went again.

And, while he bawled and bawled and bawled, the fake news reached Dancy Nancy in her woodland home and, angry that someone would break the rule, she planted a magic seed and set about growing a Gigantic Peach, using Trumplethinskin's bullcrap lies as fertilizer.

You see, Trumplethinskin hated fruit. And Dancy Nancy reckoned if she could get the massive piece of fruit close enough, it would suck him inside, after which the big bulging bag of magic beans (which really belonged to everyone anyway) could be shared with all the good and gentle folk of *Not Far Far Away Enough*.

Never again would Trumplethinskin be able to steal the realms-folks' magic beans, or have stupid ideas, like the time he wanted to use brooms to sweep away all the leaves in the woods, or his stupidest idea of all: poking Ali Khafar with a rocket and making him, along with many rulers in the Lands of the East, as mad as a sack of wasps.

"It's not fair," Trumplethinskin said, and sulked when he heard about her plan. "I haven't done anything wrong," he cried like a simpering, softy snowflake.

"Well, I did. But I am saying that I didn't, even though there is a scroll quoting exactly what I said, and did—but it's not fair, so that means I didn't say it, or ask it, or do it, or do anything . . . even though Dancy Nancy has proof."

Now, as you can see, Trumplethinskin was rambling on a bit. But, in general, most realms-folk found it hard to make heads or tails of anything Trumpthinskin told them—and they couldn't believe a single word of it, either. For someone who was *"as thick as all the short planks in the realm,"* he really was good at telling lies . . .

. . . well, he was good at telling them, but absolutely terrible at not being found out.

So, down the road Dancy Nancy went, rolling the freshly grown Gigantic Peach towards Trumplethinskin's second—at least for now—home at the Bigly Big White House (white being Trumple-thinskin's favorite color).

When she reached the front door, the Tight-fisted Turtle, Hennity Bennity, and Chucky Dollson were standing in her way:

"You cannot give Trumplethinskin that Gigantic Peach," they said in unison, as if they'd already planned what to say beforehand.

"Why not? He has broken the most important rule in all the land."

They put on their thinking faces. It looked painful. They mumbled, chatted together, and then finally, as if having a magnificent revelation, they said—in unison again, may I add:

"Because we don't like it, and that's just that."

And so, from that day forward, the Gigantic Peach sat outside the Bigly Big White House (white being Trumplethinskin's favorite color), always reminding Trumplethinskin that he really did break the most important rule in all the land, but also that he didn't care because—although he didn't have a proper throne yet—as long as they could continue dipping their grubby fingers into the big bulging bag of magic beans, Tight-fisted Turtle, Hennity Bennity, Chucky Dollson, and all of Trumplethinskin's make-believe friends would say anything, mostly lies, to pretend Trumplethinskin was indeed the King of *Not Far Far Away Enough*, and that they, at least, could live happily ever after.

Except, that was, for the ones who were banished to the deepest darkest dungeon, having been discovered telling lies on Trumplethinskin's behalf.

Just like he'd said about being in bed with Stormilocks, Trumplethinskin claimed he never knew them, even though he did, and very well indeed.

But that, yet again—like a massive, ever-growing mound of malevolence— is another story entirely.

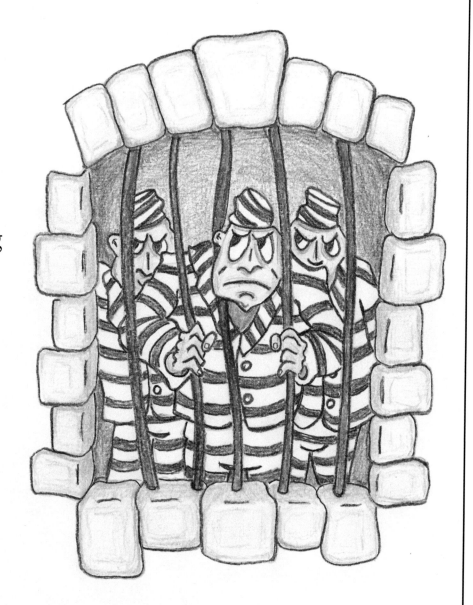

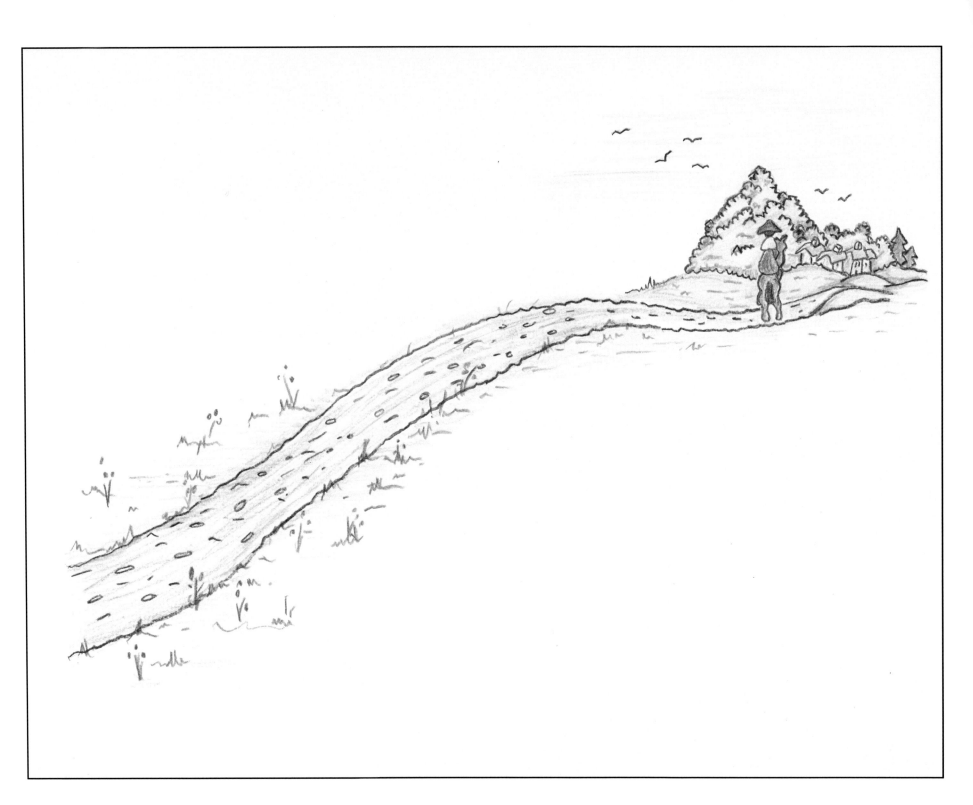

ABOUT THE AUTHOR

Martin Treanor is an author and illustrator—which didn't really need saying, because he writes and illustrates all the Trumplethinskin books. He likes coffee, cake, and cake—doesn't live anywhere snazzy but he did write two other cool books: *The Silver Mist* and *Dark Creed*. He also wrote a load of short stories too . . . oh, and illustrated some other stuff.
He likes cake.

More at: *www.MartinTreanor.com*
Martin Treanor is represented by
DRPZ™ [www.drpz.net]

Look for our thin-skinned "hero" in
Trumplethinskin and the Wizard Bonespurs and
Trumplethinskin in the Land of UcK!

For more information about this Very Stable Genius, please visit:

TheTalesOfTrumplethinskin.com
MartinTreanor.com
ANiceCuppaTea.com

@TrumpleTales

TINY HANDS

PRESS

RATCATCHERS

Ye Olde Dating Service for Fickle Folk

NAME: Trumplethinskin (third attempt)
OCCUPATION: Mega-super throne aficionado and super-duper accumulator of magic beans
LIKES: Magic beans, thrones, golden toilets, and speaking about himself in the third person
DISLIKES: People who blame Trumplethinskin for things he did
BEST QUALITY: Not taking the blame—for anything
WORST QUALITY: None—Trumplethinskin really is the bestest best at everything
FAVORITE FOOD: Still definitely beautiful chocolate cake
FAVORITE THING: Trumplethinskin

PROFILE:

This is Trumplethinskin's third go at writing a profile—his previous attempts are still awaiting a single response. But the deep state elite obviously don't want Trumplethinskin to share his being absolutely brilliant with the world. Trumplethinskin still lives in *Not Far Far Away Enough* and will, one day, definitely be king of the world. His roly-poly belly is just awesome. His beautiful orange face looks like the promise of summer. Get with me—er, I mean, Trumplethinskin—and I'll . . . *he'll* show you the best single second of your life—down again on the previous two estimates, due to the stress of having to deal with the deep state elite who live only in Trumplethinskin's mind. Yet again, no elves, hobgoblins, or pixies—as I . . . er, *he* only makes dodgy deals with those. Oh, and definitely no one who eats vegetables or fruit. Trumplethinskin hates fruit.

Lightning Source UK Ltd.
Milton Keynes UK
UKRC011337260721
387783UK00001BA/15

* 9 7 8 1 9 8 9 9 6 0 1 3 4 *